DIGITAL INSIDERS

VLOGGERS

BY BENJAMIN MARK SCHAEFER

Gareth Stevens
PUBLISHING

Please visit our website, www.garethstevens.com. For a free color catalog of all our high-quality books, call toll free 1-800-542-2595 or fax 1-877-542-2596.

Cataloging-in-Publication Data

Names: Schaefer, Benjamin Mark.
Title: Vloggers / Benjamin Mark Schaefer.
Description: New York : Gareth Stevens Publishing, 2020. | Series: Digital insiders | Includes glossary and index.
Identifiers: ISBN 9781538247679 (pbk.) | ISBN 9781538247693 (library bound) | ISBN 9781538247686 (6 pack)
Subjects: LCSH: Video blogs–Juvenile literature.
Classification: LCC TK5105.8867 2020 | DDC 302.23'14–dc23

First Edition

Published in 2020 by
Gareth Stevens Publishing
111 East 14th Street, Suite 349
New York, NY 10003

Designer: Sarah Liddell
Editor: Lynn Moon

Photo credits: Cover, p. 1 LightField Studios/Shutterstock.com; background texture used throughout VLADGRIN/Shutterstock.com; screen texture used throughout majcot/Shutterstock.com; p. 5 Dado Photos/Shutterstock.com; p. 7 (top) AngieYeoh/Shutterstock.com; p. 7 (bottom) fizkes/Shutterstock.com; p. 9 (webcam) PERLA BERANT WILDER/Shutterstock.com; p. 9 (action camera) supot phanna/Shutterstock.com; p. 9 (DSLR) Marcio Jose Bastos Silva/Shutterstock.com; p. 9 (camcorder) AlexLMX/Shutterstock.com; p. 11 (bottom) lev radin/Shutterstock.com; p. 13 (top) Abdie/Shuttertock.com; p. 13 (bottom) Jarretera/Shutterstock.com; p. 15 Dmytro Zinkevych/Shutterstock.com; p. 17 (top) JJFarq/Shutterstock.com; p. 17 (bottom) Casimiro PT/Shutterstock.com; p. 21 Featureflash Photo Agency/Shutterstock.com; p. 23 Atstock Productions/Shutterstock.com; p. 25 NiP STUDIO/Shutterstock.com; p. 27 (top) Prostock-studio/Shutterstock.com; p. 27 (bottom) dolphfyn/Shutterstock.com; p. 29 (top) FrameStockFootages/Shutterstock.com; p. 29 (bottom) jakkaje808/Shutterstock.com.

Printed in the United States of America

Some of the images in this book illustrate individuals who are models. The depictions do not imply actual situations or events.

CPSIA compliance information: Batch #CW20GS: For further information contact Gareth Stevens, New York, New York at 1-800-542-2595.

CONTENTS

Words in the glossary appear in **bold** type the first time they are used in the text.

VLOGGING: WHAT'S YOUR PASSION?

What do you think you could talk about for hours a week? Video games? Nature? Your family? Or maybe just your daily life? There might be hundreds, thousands, or even millions of people who would enjoy watching videos you create on this subject.

Vloggers are people who create videos and share them on social media, or websites where people communicate and form online communities. Vloggers get to pick what they want to talk about in videos for their fans, with some even getting paid to do it! It all starts with a passion, or strong interest, and excitement for something important to you.

TYPES OF VLOGS

Some of the most popular types of YouTube channels include videos on product reviews, personal vlogs where people talk about themselves and their lives, and tutorials. Tutorials teach the viewer something they didn't know, like how to ride a bike or solve a Rubik's cube!

IF YOU LIKE ARTS AND CRAFTS, YOU COULD MAKE VIDEOS ON HOW TO MAKE CREATIVE PROJECTS—LIKE SLIME!

VLOGGING HISTORY

Vlogging wouldn't be possible without YouTube. Three friends, Chad Hurley, Steve Chen, and Jawed Karim, created YouTube in 2005 as a way to share videos. Google bought YouTube in 2006 for $1.65 billion. The site grew to be the world's second most-visited website in 2017, right after Google.

Early on, YouTube added the ability to **subscribe** to channels, making it possible for vloggers to know how many fans they have. Now YouTube can tell you where fans are watching and even what devices they are using. YouTube has about 1.8 billion logged-in users every month—and even more people are believed to watch without logging in!

SMALL START

The first YouTube video was called "Me at the Zoo." It is a short video of site co-founder Jawed Karim at the San Diego Zoo. Jawed talks about the elephants behind him. You can look it up with a trusted adult! It's probably pretty different from YouTube videos you're used to.

AS OF 2018, PEOPLE WATCH ABOUT
5 BILLION HOURS OF YOUTUBE A DAY!

GETTING THE GEAR

Some people make their videos with just a smartphone, but many successful vloggers use a lot of different equipment, or gear, to make their videos stand out.

Equipment that can establish how your videos look and sound includes microphones to pick up the sound, cameras to help you get the best video, a tripod—or solid device to keep your camera stable—lighting gear, and video editing **software** to help you edit out the stuff you don't want. Once you get the hang of the basics, you can also use the software to add cool effects to your videos.

ALL ABOUT THE CAMERA

The most important tool for a vlogger is the camera. You can choose your camera based on the kind of video you want to make. For high-quality videos, you'll need a really good camera like a DSLR. If you're sitting and talking, you might just need a webcam.

TYPES OF CAMERAS

ACTION CAMERA
Can attach to objects like helmets and skateboards, or even pets

WEBCAM
Built into most computers and laptops

Good for getting started

CAMCORDER
Made mainly for filming, not for taking pictures

Usually cheaper than a DSLR

DSLR
Videos look clear and detailed

You can see exactly what you are filming on a screen called the viewfinder

DIFFERENT CAMERAS HAVE DIFFERENT USES. WHICH IS RIGHT FOR YOU?

VLOGGING PIONEERS

Some of the earliest vloggers are still creating today! Smosh is a **comedy** group that began making videos in 2005. They create short amusing scenes called "sketches." Now they have more than 20 million subscribers!

Michelle Phan started creating makeup tutorials and videos in 2006, and as of 2019, she had more than 8.8 million subscribers. Author, **activist**, and blogger Tyler Oakley started making his videos in 2006 as well, when he was 18 and in his first year of college! Tyler is famous for his positive videos about **LGBTQ+** topics.

A GOOD KIND OF "TROLLING"

Some vloggers have been able to make stuff that isn't only on YouTube! Smosh made a feature-length movie in 2015. You might have also recognize some of the voices from the movie *Trolls*, which featured the voices of vloggers Kandee Johnson and Ricky Dillon right next to big stars like Justin Timberlake.

TYLER OAKLEY, ABOVE, HAD MORE THAN 7 MILLION YOUTUBE SUBSCRIBERS AS OF 2019!

A WORLD OF CREATORS

Since the site started in 2005, YouTube has grown to around 50 million people creating and sharing content! The site now has programs for successful creators to help them grow their work. These programs have different levels for different numbers of subscribers, including Graphite (1,000, or 1k, subscribers), Opal (1k to 10k subscribers), and Bronze (10k to 100k subscribers). People who are very successful at growing their subscriber base can join the Silver level, which is for creators with more than 100,000 subscribers.

Today, there are more than 2,400 channels that have passed these numbers, with more than 1 million subscribers!

YOUTUBE STUDIOS

YouTube has its own studios for people that are successful and want to grow their followings on the site. If you have more than 10,000 subscribers, you can make your videos at these spaces in major cities such as New York and Toronto.

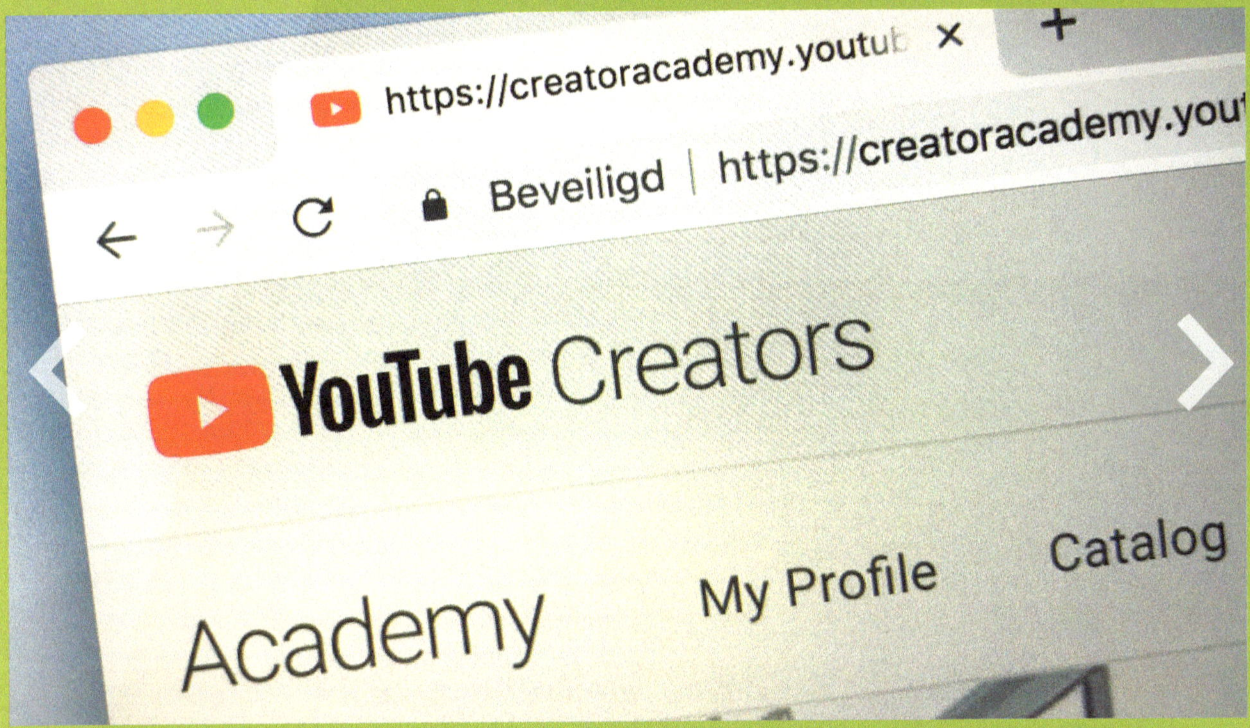

THE YOUTUBE CREATORS ACADEMY IS LIKE A SCHOOL FOR PEOPLE WHO WANT TO LEARN HOW TO VLOG BETTER!

BUT IS IT *REALLY* A JOB?

You can vlog for fun or as a real job. When you're starting out, make sure that you know how you're going to measure your success. Will it be by how many friends you make or new people you meet? Some vloggers measure success by the number of likes, dislikes, or comments. Others use the number of subscribers or how long their viewers watch a certain video, which is called "watch time."

Do you want to make a job out of vlogging? In that case, you will need to measure your success the way the pros do—by the **revenue** from partnerships, **sponsors**, and clicks.

HOW ELSE CAN YOU MAKE MONEY?

Sometimes YouTube shares revenue with their creators—to be considered, you need to enable a "monetization" feature and connect an account through the program AdSense. Other vloggers make money by "cost per click" or "cost per view" advertising. It's just what it sounds like—you get paid for either the number of clicks on the ad or the number of ad views.

HOW WOULD YOU WANT TO MEASURE YOUR SUCCESS? IT'S IMPORTANT TO HAVE A PLAN.

THE FUTURE OF SMALLTUBERS

Recent changes to YouTube's monetization policies have made many vloggers nervous. These are basically the rules about how creators can make money on YouTube. In order to join the Partner Program and make money, creators now need to reach 1,000 subscribers and 4,000 hours of watch time. This makes it harder for Smalltubers, or vloggers with smaller numbers of fans, to make vlogging their job. In the future these policies may change.

Vloggers are speaking up about their thoughts on YouTube's policies. Vloggers will need to know the policies of the sites they want to use before starting their channels.

SPONSORED RULES

Some creators get in trouble for not following the rules of the FTC, or Federal Trade Commission. By not clearly saying that their videos are sponsored, or promoting certain products, they violate YouTube and FTC policies. Future vloggers have to be aware of these rules as paid content becomes more popular.

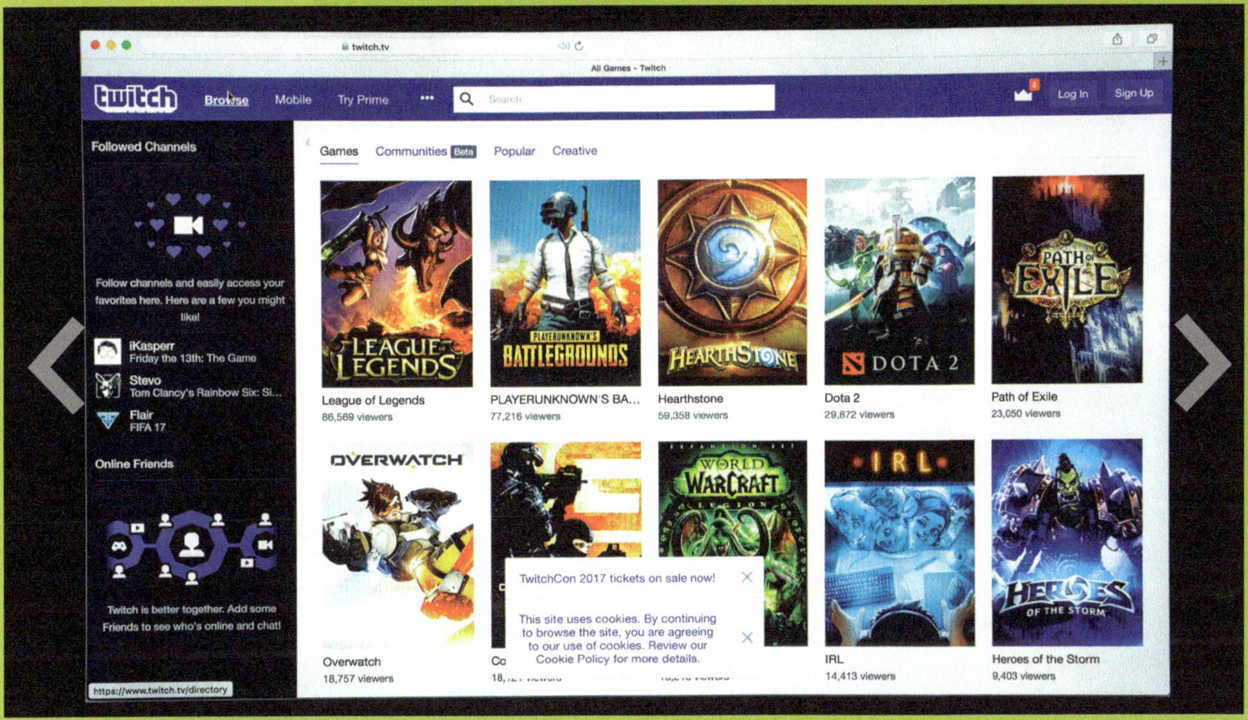

THE WEBSITE TWITCH IS ANOTHER CHOICE FOR VLOGGERS WHO FILM THEMSELVES PLAYING VIDEO GAMES.

WHERE TO FIND PEOPLE

A lot of vloggers post content on other forms of social media—not just YouTube and Twitch! You can pick one site where you want to share your videos or share them out across many different forms of social media. It's important to know the demographics, or types of people, you want to reach.

For example, if you want to make short videos for teens, you should use social media that is most popular with that age range. Since 72 percent of 13 to 17-year-olds in the United States used Instagram in 2018, that might be a good place for you to start sharing!

PAY ATTENTION TO FACEBOOK, TOO!

Some people upload their videos to Facebook, since videos start playing **automatically** as users scroll through their **news feed**. When people are looking to see what their friends are talking about, they might come across a vlogger's video. If it grabs their attention, they might subscribe to or follow the vlogger!

COMPARING MONTHLY SOCIAL MEDIA USER NUMBERS IN 2018

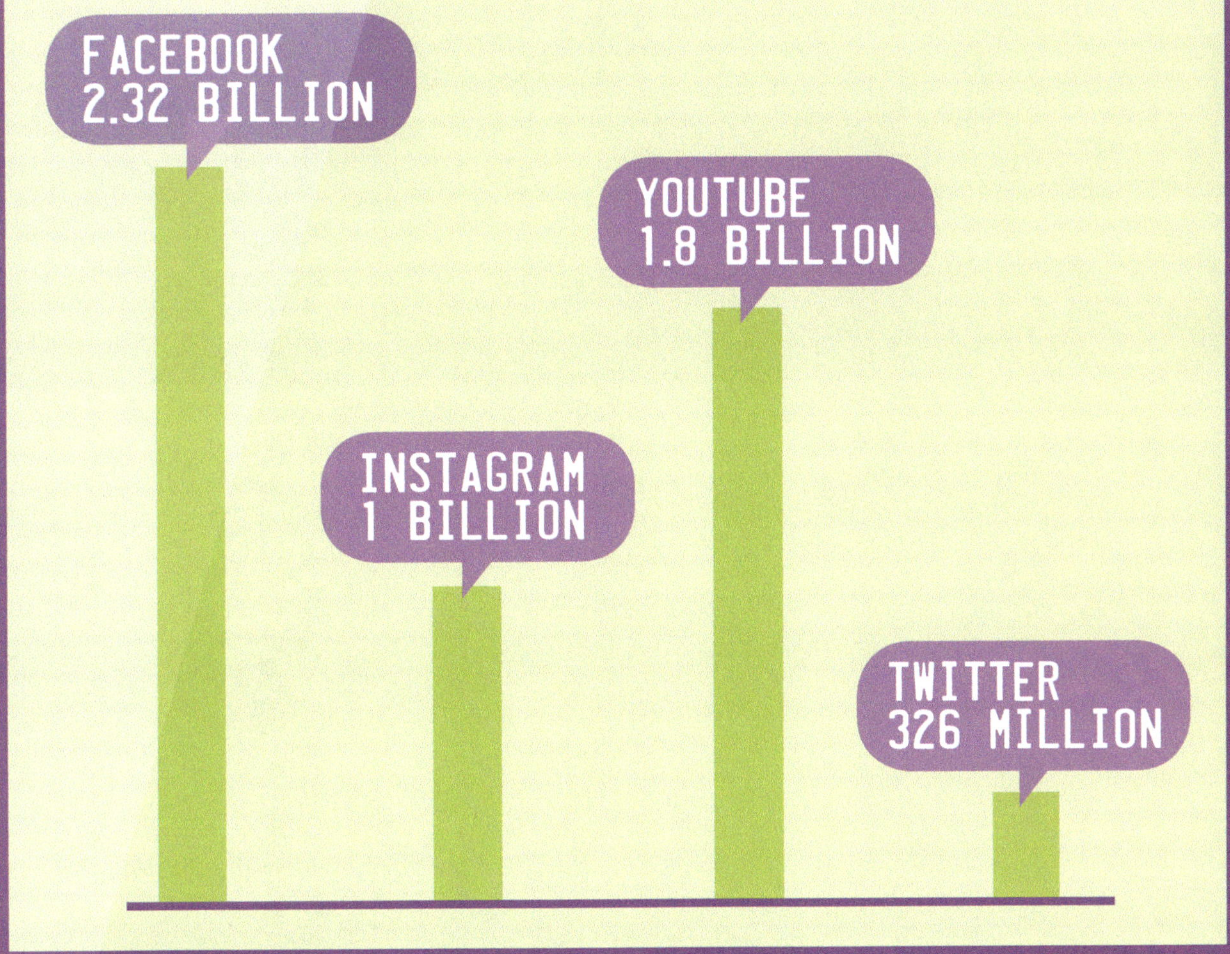

IN 2018, INSTAGRAM REACHED ABOUT 1 BILLION USERS WORLDWIDE! THAT YEAR IT ALSO ANNOUNCED IGTV, WHICH IS AIMED AT ALLOWING USERS TO SHARE LONGER VIDEOS LIKE YOUTUBE.

A KID, JUST LIKE YOU!

Even kids can be vloggers! In fact, one of the most successful vloggers around is Ryan from Ryan ToysReview. Ryan's parents started filming his toy reviews in 2015. Now he has more than 19 million subscribers! In 2018, Ryan made over $22 million dollars at just 7 years old. He was the top paid YouTuber of the year!

Ryan is very active on YouTube, posting new videos and toy reviews nearly every day. Now Ryan has gone from reviewing toys to being the inspiration for toys! Wal-Mart now sells a line of toys called Ryan's World, based on his channel.

KIDS ONLINE

Other younger YouTubers include EvanTubeHD, Kids' Toys, and Ethan Gamer. They focus on stuff that kids care about, like video games, cool toys, and their daily lives. Studies show young people are watching less regular TV and are watching more online videos. In 2018, 13 to 24-year-olds watched about 12 hours of video online per week.

THE YOUTUBE KIDS APP CAN HELP YOU AND YOUR PARENTS FIND SAFE AND FUN CHANNELS FOR KIDS UNDER 13.

INFLUENCE IS EVERYTHING!

Because Ryan's fans love him so much, he has something called "influence." Influence is the idea that you and your content could shape how people look at the world. Companies use influencers to help advertise their products to a **target** demographic.

When promoting these products or services, influencers are paid. They need to disclose, or share, that they were paid. YouTubers often disclose that a video is sponsored by writing #ad or #sponsored in the video title, or by talking about it in the video itself. Product reviews, how-to guides, and unboxing videos are popular videos for influencers to do.

#SPONSORED

Many companies now look to vloggers and influencers to reach people. Recent studies found that about 63 percent of people age 13 to 24 trust the opinion of a vlogger over a celebrity. What do you think? Do you believe a vlogger's opinion when you watch a sponsored video?

ADVERTISEMENTS AREN'T JUST ON BILLBOARDS ANYMORE! THEY CAN BE HARDER TO SPOT ONLINE—SUCH AS WHEN A VLOGGER IS PAID TO SAY GOOD THINGS ABOUT A PRODUCT.

VIDEOS CAN CHANGE THE WORLD!

More than half of people prefer watching videos online to regular TV, and it's predicted, or expected, that half of all people under 32 will not be paying to watch regular TV by 2025. The internet is growing, and growing fast! Creators have recognized this and have started making webseries, or shows that are only online. These are different from YouTube vlogs as they often have a **script** and actors.

Some webseries have even been made into regular TV shows, like *The Annoying Orange*! This story of a rude talking orange began on YouTube in 2009 and went on to be a Cartoon Network show.

THAT'S A LOT OF PEOPLE!

About 1/3 of all people on the internet use YouTube or have watched YouTube videos in the past. The number of YouTube users is expected to rise to about 1.9 billion in 2021—that's more people than in the most populous country in the world, China!

YOUTUBE IS THE SECOND LARGEST SEARCH ENGINE ON THE WEB!

SAFETY IS KEY

It's important to know the rules of the site that you want to use to host your vlog, or to store all of its information online. Many have an age requirement, which means you need to be at least a certain age to use the site.

You can open a YouTube account for watching and making videos with your parents' permission, or okay, if you're at least 13. It's important to protect your personal data, or facts about yourself. The site Vimeo also requires you to be at least 13 years old to make an account in the United States.

YOUR DATA IS YOU!

It can be a lot of fun to join the vlogging community online with a trusted adult's permission, but it's important to keep your personal data safe! Here are some things you should not share online:

- Your full name
- Birthday and age
- Home address
- Passwords
- Name of your school

EACH SITE HAS DIFFERENT RULES, AND IT'S IMPORTANT TO TALK TO YOUR PARENTS IF YOU WANT TO START YOUR OWN CHANNEL.

HOW TO GET STARTED

Before you start filming your vlog, it's important to make sure you've done your homework. You could borrow books from the library or ask your parents if you can go online and find some vloggers that you like. If you think you have something to say, write down some possible video topics and think about a personal brand, or style.

The world of vlogging keeps getting bigger. About 300 hours of YouTube videos are uploaded to the site every minute. Who knows? The videos you make might be the next **viral** hit or help you to become an influencer for the future!

LESSONS LEARNED

A lot of vloggers have even written their own books with the lessons they've learned. You can check out *Kid President's Guide to Being Awesome!* The Kid President, Robby Novak, teaches readers how to be nicer in the world, with lessons he's learned from making his YouTube videos and people he's met.

THERE HAVE BEEN A LOT OF KID-FRIENDLY BOOKS WRITTEN ON HOW TO BECOME A VLOGGER.

GLOSSARY

activist: one who acts strongly in support of or against an issue or cause

automatically: happening on its own

comedy: a movie, play, book, or other form of media meant to make people laugh

LGBTQ+: stands for the lesbian, gay, bisexual, transgender, and queer (or questioning) community

news feed: a list of updates on your Facebook homepage from friends and other connections

revenue: money that comes from the sale of goods or services

script: a written plan for a show

software: a computer code, or program, that instructs, or tells, the computer what to do

sponsor: a person, business, or organization that gives money to a creator in exchange for advertisement. Also, to provide money to a creator in exchange for advertisement.

subscribe: to follow a user or organization online, for free or for payment in advance

target: a group that a person or company is trying to sell something to or influence

viral: something that becomes popular rapidly online

FOR MORE INFORMATION

BOOKS

Birley, Shane. *How to be a Blogger and Vlogger in 10 Easy Lessons*, Lake Forest, CA: Walter Foster Jr., 2016.

Tashjian, Janet. *My Life as a YouTuber*, New York, NY: Henry Holt & Co, 2018.

Willoughby, Nick. *Making YouTube Videos: Star in Your Own Video!*, Hoboken, NJ: John Wiley & Sons, 2019.

WEBSITES

YouTube Creators
creatoracademy.youtube.com/page/home
A place where you can learn about YouTube and get lessons from successful vloggers.

Common Sense Media
www.commonsensemedia.org/blog/the-kid-youtube-stars-your-kids-love
Find real-life kid vloggers to start watching!

ParentInfo
parentinfo.org/article/a-parents-guide-to-vlogging-what-you-need-to-know
A guide for families and parents looking to get into vlogging.

Publisher's note to educators and parents: Our editors have carefully reviewed these websites to ensure that they are suitable for students. Many websites change frequently, however, and we cannot guarantee that a site's future contents will continue to meet our high standards of quality and educational value. Be advised that students should be closely supervised whenever they access the internet.

INDEX